Parent's Introduction

We Both Read is the first series of books designed to invite parents and children to share the reading of a story by taking turns reading aloud. This "shared reading" innovation, which was developed in conjunction with early reading specialists, invites parents to read the more sophisticated text on the left-hand pages, while children are encouraged to read the right-hand pages, which have been written at one of three early reading levels.

Reading aloud is one of the most important activities parents can share with their child to assist their reading development. However, *We Both Read* goes beyond reading *to* a child and allows parents to share reading *with* a child. *We Both Read* is so powerful and effective because it combines two key elements in learning: "showing" (the parent reads) and "doing" (the child reads). The result is not only faster reading development for the child, but a much more enjoyable and enriching experience for both!

Most of the words used in the child's text should be familiar to them. Others can easily be sounded out. An occasional difficult word will be first introduced in the parent's text, distinguished with **bold lettering**. Pointing out these words, as you read them, will help familiarize them to your child. You may also find it helpful to read the entire book aloud yourself the first time, then invite your child to participate on the second reading. Also note that the parent's text is preceded by a "talking parent" icon: ⌒ ; and the child's text is preceded by a "talking child" icon: ⌒ .

We Both Read books is a fun, easy way to encourage and help your child to read — and a wonderful way to start your child off on a lifetime of reading enjoyment!

We Both Read: About Pets

Use of photographs provided by Getty Images
© copyright 2002.

We Both Read® is a trademark of Treasure Bay, Inc.

Published by Treasure Bay, Inc.
17 Parkgrove Drive
South San Francisco, CA 94080 USA

PRINTED IN SINGAPORE

Library of Congress Control Number: 2002103855

Hardcover ISBN: 1-891327-41-0
Paperback ISBN: 1-891327-42-9

FIRST EDITION

We Both Read® Books
Patent No. 5,957,693

Visit us online at:
www.webothread.com

About Pets

By Sindy McKay

TREASURE BAY

 Dogs, cats, fish, birds, lizards, rats—**pets** are everywhere! They come in all different shapes, sizes and colors.

1

Pets can be big.

Pets can be small.

Pets may have lots of **nice** fluffy fur or they may be silky-smooth and shiny. Some pets have scales and some have wings. There are pets with gills and pets with shells.

Can you think of a pet that has a shell?

 This is a turtle.

Turtles are **nice** pets.

Different pets have different needs.

Birds need a cage to sleep in, but most cats **sleep** anywhere they want to. A dog must be fed every day, but some snakes only eat once a week.

Good pet owners know what's best for their pet.

Cats like to **sleep** in the sun.

According to some sources, cats are the world's most popular pets. Maybe that's because cats are so easy to care for.

Cats don't seem to mind being left alone while their owners are away at school or work. They can also be very loving and will **purr** contentedly while curled up in your lap.

A cat has soft fur.

It may **purr** if you pet it.

Some people say that dogs are the most popular pets in the world. That could be because there are so many different kinds of dogs to choose from. Or it might just be because a **puppy** is too doggone cute to resist!

 A **puppy** is a lot of fun to play with!

Dogs and cats may be the two most common household pets, but there are many other animals that make great pets as well. Some other favorite four-legged friends are rats, hamsters, rabbits, guinea pigs, lizards, turtles, and pigs.

This girl has a big
pig for a pet.

 Not all pets have four legs. Many people choose birds as pets, while others might choose **fish** or one of several species of snakes.

 **Fish** make good pets.
Cats like them, too!

 Pet owners try to spend as much time as possible with their pets and many will **talk** to them the same way they **talk** to a good friend.

 Birds love to sing.

Some birds can even **talk.**

16

The variety of pets available is vast and wonderful. But no matter what animal you choose as a pet, it must be well cared for and **loved**.

 This dog **loves** to ride in the car.

 Owning a pet is a big responsibility. An animal that has become a pet cannot take care of itself. It is the owner's responsibility to provide the right food for their pet along with plenty of fresh water to **drink.**

This is NOT a good way to get a **drink!**

 Some pets like to eat the same **food** we eat. However, feeding "people food" to a pet is not a good idea. Pets need to eat special food that has been made just for them.

 Some dogs beg for **food.**
Some kids beg for food, too!

 Another important aspect of caring for a pet is making sure it gets enough exercise.

Goldfish can take care of getting their own exercise, but cats enjoy playing with toys. Just rolling a ball of yarn across the room can keep a cat busy for a long time.

Dogs love to play.

They love to run and jump.

Regular visits to the veterinarian will help assure that your pet stays healthy. A veterinarian can advise you on the right diet and exercise to keep your pet **happy** and give any necessary shots or medicine to prevent disease.

A well pet is a **happy** pet.

 Most pets require some kind of bathing and grooming. Many need regular haircuts and **baths,** and some may need to have their nails clipped and their teeth brushed.

Big dogs use big tubs for their **baths**.

28

 Having a place to call home is important for every kind of pet. Birds need a large, clean cage of their very own. Fish **live** in an aquarium. Many reptiles and snakes need a special enclosure with a heater to keep their body temperatures steady.

This dog likes to **live** in the house.

 One of the most important things a pet needs to thrive is the time and affection of its owner.

Give your pet a big hug.
It feels good.

 If you are thinking of getting a new pet, it's a good idea to spend some time deciding what kind of pet is right for you.

Consider how much time you have to spend with the animal and how much money you are willing to spend on its care and upkeep.

A dog or cat makes
a good pet.

So does a frog.

   Few things are **cuter** than a puppy, but a puppy can be a real handful! You might want to think about choosing an older animal that's already been trained.

If you're not going to be home much, consider getting two pets so they can keep each other company.

One dog is cute.

Two dogs are **cuter!**

 It doesn't take long for a pet to become part of our lives, and soon we wonder how we ever got along without them.

They join us at work and at **play.** They cheer us up when we're sad and share our joy when we're feeling happy.

They **play** with us.

They even sing with us.

 If we give our pets what they need, they will give back to us love and devotion and laughter.